STECK-VAUGHN

Start Smart®
Connecting Learning to Life

D1192458

Test Preparation Strategies

Consultants

Jim Ford
Training Specialist
Center for Literacy Studies
University of Tennessee
Knoxville, Tennessee

Daniele D. Flannery, Ph.D.
Associate Professor of Adult Education
Coordinator: Adult Education D.Ed. Program
The Pennsylvania State University
Capital Campus—Harrisburg

Barbara Tondre-El Zorkani
Educational Consultant
Adult and Workforce Education
Austin, Texas

Harcourt Achieve
Rigby • Saxon • Steck-Vaughn

www.HarcourtAchieve.com
1.800.531.5015

Acknowledgments

Staff Credits

Executive Editor: Ellen Northcutt
Supervising Editor: Julie Higgins
Associate Editor: Sharon Sargent
Director of Design: Scott Huber
Associate Director of Design: Joyce Spicer
Designer: Jim Cauthron
Production Manager: Mychael Ferris
Production Coordinator: Paula Schumann
Image Services Coordinator: Ted Krause
Senior Technical Advisor: Alan Klemp
Electronic Production Specialist: David Hanshaw

Cover Illustration

Joan Cunningham

Photo Credits

P. 17 John Springer Collection/CORBIS; p. 33 Photodisc.
Additional photography by Comstock Royalty Free, and Getty Images
Royalty Free.

Test Preparation Strategies
ISBN 0-7398-6010-0

Printed in the United States of America

8 9 10 11 12 0982 13 12 11

4500272570

Contents

To the Learner

Whether you took your last test a week ago or 20 years ago, this book is for you. Steck-Vaughn's *Start Smart Test Preparation Strategies* will give you strategies that will help you prepare for many types of tests. By taking tests successfully, you'll be better able to achieve your educational and life goals.

Test taking is a learned skill. The more tests you take, the more you learn about taking tests. The strategies in this book will also help you learn how to take different types of tests. You'll find strategies to use before, during, and after you take a test.

Try all of the strategies and see which ones work best for you. Your favorites will help you again and again. They will help you to do well on tests whenever they occur in your life.

As you work through this book be sure to:

- Fill out the **Identify Your Test Preparation Habits** chart on page 5. This will give you an idea of what your current test-taking habits are.
- Write down your goals in the **Set Your Test Preparation Goals** web on page 7. Setting goals and checking your progress helps you to stay motivated.
- As you read, check out the **Tips**. They provide a slightly different approach to the strategies.
- Complete the **Think About It** activities. These help you think about what you have learned. You'll also see the connection to everyday life.
- Create a **Journal**. This book is divided into four main topics. At the end of each topic, you will have the opportunity to write in your journal. Writing thoughts in your own words will help you remember what you've learned and help you track your progress.
- Review what you have learned by completing **What Works for You?** on page 47.

Identify Your Test Preparation Habits

This chart can help you learn about your current test-taking habits. As you use the strategies in this book, you may notice that your habits are changing.

For each statement, circle A (always), S (sometimes), or N (never).

Before I take a test, I . . .	always	sometimes	never
manage my study time well.	A	S	N
choose a study plan that fits my lifestyle and learning style.	A	S	N
know when I'm ready to take the test.	A	S	N
get familiar with different types of test questions.	A	S	N
When I take a test, I . . .	**always**	**sometimes**	**never**
read and understand directions.	A	S	N
know how many points each section is worth.	A	S	N
manage my time well.	A	S	N
After I take a test, I . . .	**always**	**sometimes**	**never**
think about my errors.	A	S	N
revise my study plan for next time.	A	S	N

Set Your Test Preparation Goals

Education is not the filling of a pail, but the lighting of a fire.

William Butler Yeats,
Irish poet and playwright
(1865–1939)

Think about why you want to improve your test-taking skills. Perhaps you must take a test to move up a level or two in your job. Maybe you want to take the GED and get your high school degree. Perhaps you plan to take some college-level courses and want to brush up on your test-taking skills. Explain in your own words why you want to become a better test taker.

....

....

....

....

....

....

....

Consider how improved test preparation could help you in these areas of your life.

- **Family:** How could improved test-taking skills help make your family life better?
- **Work:** How could being a better test taker help you earn a raise or a promotion?
- **Community:** What could you learn that would help you serve your community?
- **Self:** How could improved test-taking skills help you continue your education, explore an interest, or begin a new career?

Keep your goals in mind as you work through this book. In the following sections, you will start learning ways to reach your goals.

Write your goals for test preparation in the spaces below. Think about how becoming a better test taker will affect your family, your work, your community, and yourself.

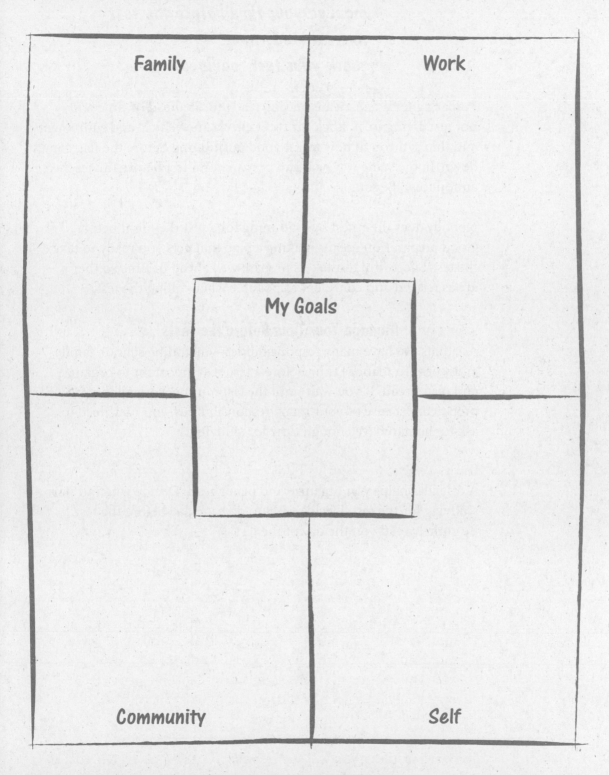

Keep your goals in mind as you work through this book.

Topic 1: Prepare for the Test

In this section, you will learn how to:

- *manage your time before the test*
- *make a study plan*
- *check your test readiness*

Preparing for a test means getting ready for it ahead of time and not just diving in. A stock car racer checks the vehicle and equipment and thinks through how to get good positioning before the flag comes down. In the same way, you can prepare for a test before the teacher announces, "Begin."

Nobody does their best by cramming for a test the night before. Good preparation means making a plan that gets you ready to take the test. Successful test takers prepare well ahead of time so they are as relaxed and confident as possible when taking the test.

Strategy 1: Manage Your Time Before the Test

As adults, we have many responsibilities—including school, family, and work. To manage time before a test, it's important to organize and plan ahead. If you wait until the last minute, you will not be well prepared. Because of your many responsibilities, you may need to ask for help to have enough time for studying.

Use a Calendar

A calendar helps you organize and plan ahead. Decide when to start studying for the test. Decide what to do each day before the test. Be entirely ready on the day of the test.

On this calendar, Justine wrote down what to do on each day leading up to the test:

S	M	T	W	Th	F	S
re-read chapter 11	re-read chapter 12	re-read chapter 13	take notes on chapter 11	take notes on chapter 12	take notes on chapter 13	go to review session, 2:00 p.m.
day off	review notes on chapter 11	review notes on chapter 12	review notes on chapter 13	write summary of chapters 11–13	business math test, rm. 410B, 10:00 a.m.	

Justine wanted lots of time to review. First, she re-read the chapters. Next, she reviewed them by taking notes. Then she reviewed her notes. Finally, she wrote a summary. By the day of the test, she knew the material very well.

Not everyone would use this same plan. One person might take notes while re-reading. Another might read a chapter one day and take notes on it the next day. There is no one right way to organize your time and plan for a test. Decide which way is best for you.

Work with a Partner

Create a pre-test plan by using your own date book, pocket calendar, or the calendar below. Imagine that you have a test in 10 days. Work backward to make a plan, writing key words in each box.

TIP
Work backward from the day of your test to schedule your time for studying.

S	M	T	W	Th	F	S
		Test Day				

Compare your plan to your partner's. How are they different? How are they the same? Are there any ideas you'd like to borrow from each other? Discuss the way your plans could help you organize your time as you prepare for a test.

Think About It
How can you better manage your time when getting ready for a big event?

....

....

Strategy 2: Make a Study Plan
You've organized your time with a schedule for studying. Now you need to make a study plan. The plan you choose will depend on what is being tested, your lifestyle, and your learning style.

Recognize Your Learning Style
Do you learn better by reading, listening, or doing? Your personal learning style will help you make a study plan that's right for you. This chart lists activities for each learning style.

Reading	Listening	Doing
• Write a summary of what you read.	• Tape class or study sessions and listen to the tape for review.	• Make your own practice tests to check your understanding.
• Read instructions rather than asking for a demonstration.	• Study with a partner.	• Act out instructions.
• Take good notes and read them later.	• Ask someone to explain what you don't understand.	• Show someone what you're learning.
• Find background material related to what you're studying.	• Read aloud material you are studying.	• Move around as you study.

For example, John is studying for his GED. His class is working on math skills this month. John likes to hear instructions and explanations. When he is learning something new, he wants to see someone demonstrate the activity.

John chooses activities from the Listening and Doing columns that he can use while studying.

John decides to study with a partner. He also decides to tape-record his class so he can listen to it at home. He schedules a meeting with his GED teacher to see her demonstrate some of the more difficult math problems. Later he will show his study partner, Bill, how to do these problems.

John's study plan looks like this:

Listening	Doing
• Tape class and listen to review. • Study with Bill on Saturday at 2:00 p.m. • Ask Mrs. Vega to demonstrate multiplying fractions again.	• Show Bill what I learned about fractions.

Try It Yourself
What activities will you choose as you study for a test? Make your own chart and post it to remind you of your study plan.

Study with Others
If it fits your learning style, studying with a partner or group can be very useful. Studying with others can help you:

- understand difficult information
- focus on what is important
- try out your ideas on others

Here are some methods that may help your study group prepare for a test.

METHOD 1: JIGSAW
Each person learns one area of the test topic. They then teach the main points of that area to the rest of the group.

METHOD 2: QUESTION AND ANSWER
Each person makes a list of 10 questions based on the test topic. Students take turns asking their questions and having different people answer them.

METHOD 3: OUTLINE
Students work by themselves to outline the topic or lessons for the test. Then they meet to compare their outlines. They support their own outlines by giving reasons for their organization.

If the same question comes up often in your group, there's a good chance it will be on the test.

Work with a Group

Choose a magazine article or a textbook chapter. As a group, choose one of the methods above—Jigsaw, Question and Answer, or Outline—to study for a "test" on the reading. After you have worked through your method, discuss what happened. Did your group's method work for you? How could it work better? Write your ideas here.

Method we used: ....

How well it worked: ....

....

What we could have done better: ....

....

....

....

TIP
There is no better way to make sure you understand material than to teach it to others.

Think About It
How can you make sure you are not distracted when studying?

....

....

Strategy 3: Check Your Test Readiness

In preparing for a test, you must think about *when* you will study. You must also decide *what* your study plan is, including *where* and *how* you will study. It also helps to look at *why* you are studying. Having a goal will help motivate you to prepare well for tests.

You'll be ready to take a test when you've:

- completed the reading and assignments
- gathered all classroom information (be sure to get material from any classes you missed)
- studied ahead of time

If you are uncertain about a specific topic on the test, get help. Focus on that area as the test day comes closer.

Use a Checklist

Aaron used the following checklist to decide if he was ready to take a test.

Test Readiness Checklist

✓ I know the most important idea or test topic.
It is *how an engine works.*

✓ I know five supporting details about the topic.
1. *Combustion happens in a closed space.*
2. *The electrical system starts the engine.*
3. *The engine is cooled by water.*
4. *A piston draws in fuel and air.*
5. *An exhaust valve lets out burned gas.*

✓ I know the format of the test. It will be
(multiple choice)   (short answer)   essay   other

✓ I am most worried about my knowledge
of *the steps of combustion.*

TIP

Get a good night's sleep and eat a good breakfast before taking a test.

Aaron now knows what to expect. He knows the major facts about the test. Aaron also knows what else he should study—the steps in combustion. This will help him do some final preparation for the test.

My Plan: Re-read Chapter 2 and write a summary of the steps of combustion.

Try It Yourself

Think about a test you expect to take in the near future. Complete this checklist. Notice where there are gaps in your readiness. Plan to become completely ready for the test.

Test Readiness Checklist

✔ I know the most important idea or test topic.

It is ....

✔ I know five supporting details about the topic.

1. ....

2. ....

3. ....

4. ....

5. ....

✔ I know the format of the test. It will be

multiple choice   short answer   essay   other

✔ I am most worried about my knowledge of ....

....

My Plan: ....

....

....

....

....

Think About It

How do you feel when you are ready to take a test? How do you feel when you are not as prepared as you'd like to be?

....

....

When You Prepare for a Test

- Manage your time before the test by organizing and planning ahead.
- Choose a study plan that fits your personal learning style.
- Check your test readiness. See what you know and work on the gaps.

Journal

Write a paragraph describing how you have prepared for tests in the past. Then write a paragraph describing how you will prepare for them now. Try to be as specific as possible when you write.

Next, look at the goals you set on page 7. Note your progress for each of your goals. If you've achieved a goal, put a check next to it and congratulate yourself!

Topic 2: **Answer Different Types of Questions**

In this section, you will learn how to:

- *answer multiple-choice questions*
- *read critically*
- *respond to true-false statements*
- *write an essay*
- *answer short-answer questions*

Remember pop quizzes? How did you like true-false exams? What did you think about multiple-choice tests?

You can help yourself to prepare for different tests by becoming familiar with some of the basic types of questions. These question types appear over and over again. You will find them both on standardized tests (GED, TABE) and on classroom tests in high school and college. Knowing what to expect from different tests can help you do better on them.

Strategy 1: **Answer Multiple-Choice Questions**

Multiple-choice tests are the easiest tests to grade. This makes them popular with instructors of large groups. On a multiple-choice test you will see a question or problem followed by four or five possible answer choices. Only one of the answer choices is correct.

Look at the following example. Circle the correct answer.

1. Solve: $45 + ? = 70$
   - (A) 5
   - (B) 15
   - (C) 25
   - (D) 35
   - (E) none of the above

For this problem, you must find the number that replaces the question mark. The answer is $45 + 25 = 70$. Did you pick (C)?

When taking a multiple-choice test, always remember:

1. Read the question carefully. Once you've picked an answer, read the question again with your answer.
2. Ask yourself whether the answer you're considering completely addresses the question. If the test answer is only partly true or is true only under certain narrow conditions, then it's probably not the right answer.
3. If you think an item is a trick question, think again. Very few tests have deceptive questions. Make sure you're not reading too much into the question. In most cases, questions are only tricky because they're not taken at face value.
4. If the question asks "which is not correct," write "NOT" next to the answers so you don't forget that you're looking for the false answer.
5. Don't speed through the test with the idea of going back to change answers later. Take time to think through each question. Your first answer will usually be the correct one. Carefully answer each question the first time you go through the exam and change only those answers that are clearly mistakes.

Eliminate Wrong Answers

On a multiple-choice test, you might not always know the correct answer. Sometimes you need to make an educated guess. A good multiple-choice question has wrong answers that are believable, but not quite right. To make an educated guess, cross off the wrong answers. This narrows your possible choices, giving you a better chance at choosing the right answer.

Look at this question and the chart on page 18.

1. *Romeo and Juliet* is about—
   (A) lovers meeting at a party
   (B) children carrying on their parents' quarrel
   (C) a trader from Verona
   (D) how hatred cannot cause tragedy
   (E) teenage lovers caught in a feud between their families

Possible Answers	What's Wrong?	Reason to Cross Off
lovers meeting at a party	too narrow	The answer covers only a small part of the reading.
children carrying on their parents' quarrel	incorrect	The answer is untrue based on the reading.
a trader from Verona	not relevant	The answer has little or nothing to do with the reading.
how hatred cannot cause tragedy	opposite	The answer is the reverse of the correct answer.
teenage lovers caught in a feud between their families	correct	Don't cross out. This is correct.

Some answers are incorrect. Others are not relevant, since they don't include the main point. Others are the opposite of the right answer. You should be able to cross off these incorrect answers pretty quickly.

Then look at the remaining answers. Some are too broad or too narrow. At first you may not know if they are correct. But one answer will be closer to the point. You can see that the other answers cover only a small part or cover too wide an area of the reading.

Work with a Partner

Answer the following multiple-choice question. Trade your answer with a partner. Talk with your partner about which answers you think are wrong and why. Discuss which answers were easy to cross off and which ones were more difficult.

1. The movie *Titanic* is based on—

    (A)   an unsinkable ship

    (B)   two people who are in love

    (C)   a huge ship that sank with many lives lost

    (D)   how weather affects sailing

    (E)   a terrible tragedy in the 20th century

Check your answer on page 48.

Use an Answer Form

On most standardized tests, such as the GED or TABE, you use a pencil to fill in the circles or ovals on an answer form. You fill in one oval as you answer each question. If you skip a question, you must skip that numbered oval, too. If possible, draw a circle around the answer in your test booklet before marking it on the answer form. Check the answer form against the test booklet to make sure you filled in the correct ovals.

1. Solve: $45 + ? = 70$
    - (A) 5
    - (B) 15
    - (C) 25
    - (D) 35
    - (E) none of the above

2. Solve: $? - 3 = 25$
    - (A) 28
    - (B) 22
    - (C) 38
    - (D) 32
    - (E) none of the above

The correct answers look like this:

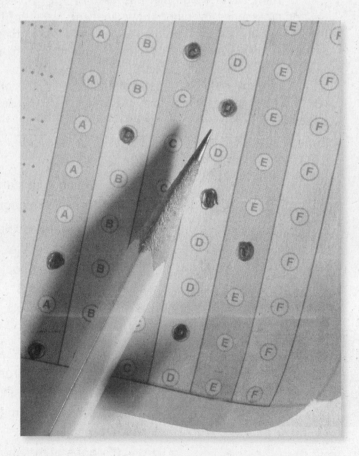

Test Yourself

Read the passage below. Then choose the best answer to each question. Mark your answers on the answer sheet on page 21. Check your answers on page 48.

There are many signs made to protect or inform people. Many of these signs do not have words. They use pictures to tell what they mean. These pictures mean the same thing around the world.

Think about a sign that has a skull and crossbones. Everyone knows that the sign means "poison." A sign like this can save someone's life.

Other signs that protect people include a road sign with a jumping deer. This sign means "wild animal crossing."

Drivers who see this sign know that they should slow down and be on the lookout.

A sign with a big question mark tells you that you can find information in that place. A sign with a fork and knife on a white circle means "restaurant." If you travel outside of the United States, you can look for those signs to find information or a place to eat.

No matter where you are, wordless signs can help you. Obey the signs, and use them to find your way.

1. According to this article, what do signs do besides inform people?

   (A) entertain people
   (B) protect people
   (C) introduce people
   (D) both A and B
   (E) none of the above

TIP
Remember to erase any stray marks on your answer sheet.

2. A picture of a deer on a sign means

   (A) wild animal crossing
   (B) railroad crossing
   (C) domestic animal crossing
   (D) restaurant
   (E) none of the above

3. Which of these might count as a
   wordless sign?

   (A) a stop sign
   (B) a street sign
   (C) a cigarette with a line through it
   (D) a sign written in Braille
   (E) none of the above

1. Ⓐ Ⓑ Ⓒ Ⓓ Ⓔ

2. Ⓐ Ⓑ Ⓒ Ⓓ Ⓔ

3. Ⓐ Ⓑ Ⓒ Ⓓ Ⓔ

Watch for Complex Answer Choices

Sometimes tests have complex answer choices that require your
complete attention. Look at each answer and see which ones are
correct—all, or some, or none. Pay close attention to these complex
answer choices.

- *None of the above*

  For this to be your answer, **none** of the answer choices can be
  correct.

- *All of the above*

  If you know that two or more answer choices are correct, this
  could be your answer. If you know that at least **one** answer choice
  is **incorrect,** this cannot be your answer.

- *Both A and B*

  This can be your answer only if **both** answer choices A and B are
  correct.

- *Neither A nor B*

  Choose this answer **only** if A is incorrect and B is incorrect, too.

When Irv took the following test he tried to pay close attention to the complex answer choices. See if you agree with his answers, which are circled in green. Check the answer key at the end.

Hint: Irv did not get all the answers right.

1. Identify the even numbers.
   A. 54
   B. 86
   C. 240
   D. 612
   E. all of the above

2. Identify the number that is a multiple of 5.
   A. 52
   B. 37
   C. 98
   D. 126
   E. none of the above

3. Identify the odd numbers.
   A. 11
   B. 12
   C. 13
   D. both A and B
   E. both A and C

4. Identify the number that is a multiple of 9.
   A. 36
   B. 54
   C. both A and B
   D. neither A nor B

Irv got number 1 right because A, B, C, and D are all even numbers—so the answer is E. He got number 2 right because neither A, B, C, nor D is a possible answer. They are not multiples of 5. So the answer is E. Irv got number 3 wrong because A is an odd number and so is C—therefore the answer is E. He got number 4 right because A is a possible answer and so is B. The answer must be C.

Try It Yourself

Circle the letter of the correct answer. Pay close attention to tricky answer choices. Check your answers on page 48.

1. Identify the words with silent letters.

   A. sleigh
   B. true
   C. rodeo
   D. both A and B
   E. both B and C

2. Identify the word that rhymes with *wharf*.

   A. half
   B. turf
   C. scarf
   D. chart
   E. none of the above

3. Identify the word that means *foolish*.

   A. reckless
   B. sensible
   C. both A and B
   D. neither A nor B

4. Identify the word(s) that names a body part.

   A. shoulder
   B. soldier
   C. solder
   D. solution
   E. all of the above

Think About It

How have you narrowed down choices in your life?

....

....

Strategy 2: Read Critically

Many tests ask you to read critically. This means you read a passage carefully, think about what it means, and answer questions about it.

Recognize the Skills Being Tested

Critical reading tests are aimed at specific reading skills. No matter what the passage is about, the questions for certain skills will be similar. This chart gives examples of questions that test each skill. When you know which skill is being tested, you can give the best answer.

Skill	Description	Sample Questions
Main Idea	summarizing paraphrasing	• *What is the best title for this passage?* • *This passage is about (What?)*
Details	recalling facts identifying names and dates	• *How old is the main character?* • *In what year did this take place?*
Cause & Effect	identifying reasons identifying results	• *Why did he perform (this action)?* • *After she (did something), what happened?*
Compare & Contrast	identifying likenesses identifying differences	• *How are the main character and the boy alike?* • *How is the boy different from the main character?*
Inference	drawing conclusions making predictions	• *If that is the case, what do you expect to happen?* • *Based on that information, which would be true?*
Author's Point of View	identifying author's opinion determining author's intent	• *What does the author think about the main character?* • *Why did the author include a character like the boy?*
Vocabulary	finding meaning from context recognizing multiple-meaning words	• *In line 10, what is the best definition of (the specific word)?* • *Which meaning of (the specific word) does the author use here?*

Work with a Group

As a group, read a short magazine article. Each person in the group should choose one type of question from the chart. Then each person should write a question about the article. See if the members of your group can answer the questions. Which questions were easiest? Which ones were harder?

TIP
Slow down when reading nonfiction passages. Summarize information in your head as you read.

....

....

....

Skim Questions

Skimming the questions before you read alerts you to the things you should watch for as you read. *Skim only the questions, not the answer choices.* When you skim questions, you save time. You don't have to go back and re-read a lot of the passage.

Maria skimmed the questions on an exam, including this one:

> 1. Why does the author include facts about trains?
>   (A) to make a point about transportation in Japan
>   (B) to contrast trains with automobiles
>   (C) to explain why he thinks planes are better
>   (D) to show transportation has changed
>   (E) none of the above

When Maria was reading the passage, she paid special attention to the part on trains. As she read about trains, she asked herself "What is the author's main point? What do these train facts add up to?"

Try It Yourself

Find a sample reading test in the test-preparation section of your library or from your school. Choose two different questions on different passages on the test.

- For question 1, read the passage first. Then answer the question.
- For question 2, skim the question before you read the passage. Then answer the question.

Which method worked better for you?

....

....

....

....

....

....

....

....

Test Yourself

Skim the questions in the boxes below and on the next page. Then read the passage. Read the questions again and choose the best answer. Check your answers on page 48.

CHICAGO—Why is Chicago called "The Windy City"? The nickname a city has can tell you a lot about that city.

Anyone who has lived in Chicago can tell you that it earns its nickname. The winds that howl off Lake Michigan in winter can knock you off your feet!

Los Angeles means "The City of Angels" in Spanish. The Spanish settled Los Angeles, and the city still has a large Spanish-speaking population.

Many cities in Europe have their own nicknames, too. Paris, France, is known as "The City of Lights." It's certainly a romantic name, but its history is also based on fact. Paris was the first city in Europe to have streetlights.

As you read the questions, think: What skill is being tested?

1. What is the best title for this passage?

    (A) U.S. and European Cities

    (B) Nicknames Around the World

    (C) Cities and Their Nicknames

    (D) Naming a New City

    (E) The Windy City and Its Neighbors

2. Which meaning of *earns* does the author use here?

    (A) totals

    (B) deserves

    (C) is paid for

    (D) secures

    (E) accepts

3. What does the author think about Paris's nickname?

   (A) It is perfect.
   (B) It is silly.
   (C) It is incorrect.
   (D) It is impractical.
   (E) It is both romantic and factual.

Think About It

How can you start improving your vocabulary today?

....

....

Strategy 3: Respond to True-False Statements

True-false statements have only two possible answers. For each statement, you have a 50 percent chance of being right.

When answering true-false statements

- Read the statements very carefully.
- Don't expect to see a pattern such as T F T F T F.
- Watch for "absolute" statements. Words such as *all, always, never,* or *none* often lead to a false answer. Usually the statement is true only in some cases, and the "absolute" words make it false.

Look at the statements below. Circle *T* if the statement is true. Circle *F* if the statement is false.

1. School bus drivers work Mondays through Fridays.   T   F
2. All bus drivers work Mondays through Fridays.   T   F
3. It never snows in Florida.   T   F
4. It rarely snows in Florida.   T   F

Number 1 is true because generally bus drivers work each day of the school week. But see how the word *all* changes the meaning of number 2. With *all*, number 2 is false: Not necessarily all of the drivers work each day. The word *never* makes number 3 false. The word *rarely* is more reasonable. It makes number 4 true.

Try It Yourself

Write a statement you know is true. Then use the word *all*, *always*, *never*, or *none* to change the true statement to a false statement.

....

....

Test Yourself

Read the passage below. Then read the numbered statements that follow. Circle *T* if the statement is true. Circle *F* if the statement is false.

SHIPPING INFORMATION:

- All prices include FREE SHIPPING if the order is $50 or more and is being shipped within the continental U.S.

- For orders under $50, please add a $3.95 shipping fee.

- Orders under 100 pounds shipped to Alaska, Hawaii, Puerto Rico, Guam, or the Virgin Islands are shipped Parcel Post. Items over 100 pounds are shipped freight.

- No C.O.D.s. We accept company checks, personal checks, VISA, MasterCard, American Express, or Discover.

- Most orders are shipped within 48 hours.

1. You can pay for your order by check.   T   F
2. Orders over $50 always have free shipping.   T   F
3. Light items shipped to Guam are sent Parcel Post.   T   F
4. C.O.D.s are never accepted.   T   F
5. Some orders to Alaska are shipped freight.   T   F

Check your answers on page 48.

Think About It

How will careful reading help you with your bills and contracts?

....

....

Strategy 4: Write an Essay

Certain test questions ask you to write out your answers in an essay. These can be as short as a paragraph or as long as a few pages. The essay "prompt" tells you what you need to write about. You may also hear the prompt called an "essay question" or "the topic."

Read the Prompt

Carefully read the prompt. It has all the information you need. The prompt should tell you *what* to write. It may also tell you *how much* to write or *for whom* to write.

TIP
Check each paragraph against the prompt as you write.

Charles used the information in the prompt below to decide what he was supposed to write. He underlined the key points of the prompt so that he knew what to do.

1. Choose <u>two forms of exercise</u>. Write <u>a short essay</u> that <u>compares</u> and <u>contrasts</u> the two. Tell <u>who might benefit</u> from each form of exercise.

It helps to put the assignment into your own words. You can jot them down or just keep them in your head. Charles thought of the assignment this way:

> I need to write a <u>short essay,</u> so about <u>two paragraphs.</u>
> I need to <u>pick two kinds of exercise.</u> I should write how they
> are the <u>same</u> and <u>different.</u> I also have to think about <u>who might</u>
> <u>benefit</u> from the exercises and write that down.

These tips will help you write a better essay.

IF the instructions say "explain why" or "state the reasons,"
→ THEN write about causes or reasons.

IF the instructions say "explain the effects," → THEN write about what happens.

IF the instructions say "discuss the pros and cons," → THEN explain the plusses and minuses.

IF the instructions say "describe," → THEN tell what something is like and what its qualities are.

$\boxed{\text{IF}}$ the instructions say "compare and contrast," ⟶ $\boxed{\text{THEN}}$ explain how things are alike and different.

$\boxed{\text{IF}}$ the instructions say "state your opinion" or "express your view," ⟶ $\boxed{\text{THEN}}$ tell what you think about an issue and why.

Try It Yourself

Read this prompt carefully and underline key information.

> Choose a famous musician or writer. In an essay of 100 words or less, tell why you think this person is a good role model for children.

Restate this prompt in your own words.

....
....
....
....

Repeat Key Words

It's a good idea to repeat key words from the prompt in your essay. Choose the words and use them right away in your introduction. This starts you off with a connection to the assignment. It can also help you to focus on the main points you want to cover.

Allison read this prompt for her essay exam. She then underlined key words.

> SUVs are very popular cars today. However, many people think they should be banned. In a short essay, explain some of the "plusses" and "minuses" about these cars.

Allison started her essay with this introduction. See how she used the underlined words from the prompt.

> SUVs are everywhere in America today. These cars are both loved and hated as they crowd our streets. SUVs have many "plusses" and "minuses" that draw these strong opinions. Some people even think they should be banned.

Try It Yourself

Underline key words in each prompt below. Use the words to write an introduction that's two or three sentences long.

1. "People get the news in many different ways. Reading the newspaper is better than watching TV." Write a short essay that responds to this statement.

   ....

   ....

2. Using examples, describe some differences between professional basketball and college basketball.

   ....

   ....

Think About It
How do you focus on what is "key" in your life?

....

....

Strategy 5: Answer Short-Answer Questions

A short-answer question does not give you answer choices. To answer, you must write a few words or a sentence or two. Use the question as your guide to answer correctly.

Restate Questions as Statements

A simple way to tackle these questions is by turning them into statements. You will then have a clear idea of what to write. By finishing the statement, you can answer the question in a complete sentence.

Carlos restated the following questions this way:

Question: When did dinosaurs first appear on Earth?
Restatement: Dinosaurs first appeared on Earth (when?).

Question: What are the stages of butterfly growth?
Restatement: The stages of butterfly growth are (what?).

Question: Where would you expect to find sea slugs?
Restatement: You would expect to find sea slugs (where?).

Try It Yourself

Restate each question below as a statement. If you know the answer, complete each statement.

1. When did the Korean War take place?

....

....

TIP

Check if your test requires complete sentences. If so, capitalize and punctuate your answers correctly.

2. Who was the first president of the United States?

....

....

3. Where does the current president of the United States live?

....

....

Check your answers on page 48.

Restate "Why?" Questions as Statements

Questions that begin with the word "Why" can usually be restated using the word "because." By using the word "because," you figure out the answer to the question.

Roland used "because" to restate questions this way:

Question: Why do most dentists encourage flossing?
Restatement: Most dentists encourage flossing because (why?).

Question: Why is registering to vote important?
Restatement: Registering to vote is important because (why?).

The word "because" helped Roland to answer the questions completely.

Work with a Partner

Write three "why" questions about safety, such as "Why should you wear goggles when sawing?" or "Why should you not eat raw eggs?" Trade questions with your partner. Use the word "because" to restate each question and answer it aloud.

....

....

....

....

....

Test Yourself

Read the passage below. Answer each question that follows on page 34 in a complete sentence.

Snuff It Out!

Many people think that smokeless tobacco is safe. Nothing could be further from the truth. Knowing the facts about smokeless tobacco can keep you from a long struggle with addiction and bad health.

Snuff and chewing tobacco are two kinds of smokeless tobacco. You may have seen baseball players with bulging cheeks. They often have wads of chewing tobacco between their teeth and gums.

Oral cancer is one of the dangerous side effects of smokeless tobacco. Cancers of the lip, tongue, and gums are common, even in young people who chew tobacco or dip snuff.

Smokeless tobacco can also damage the teeth. It exposes the roots of the teeth and wears down their surfaces. This leads to rotten teeth.

The only way people can avoid the dangers of smokeless tobacco is to stop using it. The longer they use it, however, the harder it is to stop.

1. How can smokeless tobacco damage teeth?

   ....

2. Where do smokeless tobacco users often develop cancers?

   ....

3. Why do some baseball players have bulging cheeks?

   ....

Check your answers on page 48.

Think About It
How could the "restating" strategy help you answer questions that people ask you on the job?

....

....

When You Answer Different Types of Questions
- Cross off wrong answers on a multiple-choice test.
- Skim questions before you read passages.
- Watch for "absolute" statements in true-false tests.
- Use key words from prompts in the introduction of your essay.
- Restate short-answer questions as statements.

Journal
Write a paragraph about the strategies from this chapter that you think were most helpful to you. Explain how you might use these strategies in your everyday life as well. Try to be as specific as possible when you write.

Next, look at the goals you set on page 7. Note your progress for each of your goals. If you've achieved a goal, put a check next to it and congratulate yourself!

Topic 3: Take the Test

In this section, you will learn how to:

- *preview question types and directions*
- *manage your time during the test*

You've prepared for the test. You've practiced answering different types of test questions. Now you're sitting in a room with a test booklet in front of you.

You'll do better on the test if you quickly preview it before jumping in. You'll figure out what kinds of questions are coming up. You'll see what parts are worth more points. It is also important to manage your time during the test.

Strategy 1: Preview Question Types and Directions

Even though you are prepared for your test, it's good to "look before you leap." It's wise to look at the question types and questions before you put pencil to paper.

Preview the Test

Before you begin, write your name on your test paper or booklet. Next, skim through the test. If the test is in sections and you are limited to one section at a time, skim the first section.

Using a quick mental checklist will give you an overall feel for the test:

- Are all of the pages there?
- What kinds of questions are being asked?
- How much reading is there?
- How many points are the questions or parts worth?
- How much time will this take?

After you go through your mental checklist, you can decide on a plan for taking the test. This will help you do a better job.

Before Keisha starts her test, she runs through her mental checklist. Then she develops her plan for the test.

Keisha's Checklist

- ✿ Am I missing any pages? *no*
- ✿ Is the test multiple-choice or short-answer? *25 short answers*
- ✿ Are there any essay questions? How many? *no*
- ✿ Is there a lot of reading to do? *a medium amount*
- ✿ Is one section or question type worth more points than another? *no*
- ✿ Are the sections timed? *I have 1 hour for the whole test.*

> I have an hour to do 25 short-answer questions. I can take up to 2 minutes each, and have time at the end to check things over.

Try It Yourself
Use a mental checklist to make a plan for taking a test. Write your plan below.

....

....

....

....

Read the Directions
Before you begin writing down any answers, read the directions for every part of the test. See exactly what the directions are asking for. If you have any questions, *raise your hand and ask*. If you are taking a standardized test and cannot ask questions, leave that section until the end. Then read the directions again and figure them out as best as you can.

Look at the following IF-THEN diagram. This will give you clues as to what to do.

Essay Test

IF there are several essay questions, —→ THEN do you have to answer all of them?

IF there is one essay question, —→ THEN is there a word limit?

Short-Answer Test

IF you must answer in your own words, —→ THEN do you have to use complete sentences?

Multiple-Choice Test

IF there are several answer choices, —→ THEN are you allowed to choose more than one?

IF the entire test is multiple-choice, —→ THEN should you answer on a separate answer form?

IF it is a math test, —→ THEN are you supposed to show your work?

Try It Yourself
Read these test directions. Write down exactly what you are supposed to do, using your own words. Use the IF-THEN diagram to help you. (Do not actually answer the questions.)

1. On the back of this sheet of paper, write three paragraphs. Tell step-by-step how to address an envelope.

   I am supposed to ....

   ....

2. Use a separate sheet of paper to answer one of these three essay questions.

   I am supposed to ....

   ....

3. Answer questions 1–10 in complete sentences.

   I am supposed to ....

   ....

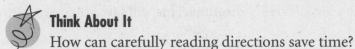

Think About It
How can carefully reading directions save time?

....

....

Strategy 2: Manage Your Time During the Test

Most tests have time limits. For example, you might be given three hours for each section of a standardized test. In the classroom, you may have one class period to take a test.

You want to avoid hearing "Pencils down" when you still have a page or two left to complete. By managing your time during the test, you will do better on it.

Managing your time will depend on:

- the kinds of questions on the test
- the point values of questions on the test
- the amount of time you are given to take the test

Understand Point Values

The number of points each test question is worth is called the *point value*. Point values vary for different tests.

- Type 1: Every question is worth the same number of points.
  On these tests, it makes sense to answer all the easy questions first. Then go back to the more difficult ones.

- Type 2: Different sections have different point values.
  If a single essay question counts for 50 percent of your grade, plan your time carefully. Save at least half of the time for the essay question.

- Type 3: Questions are easy at the beginning. They get harder as you continue.
  The more difficult questions may be worth more points than the easier ones. Pace yourself so that you have time to answer the more difficult questions.

- Type 4: Some standardized tests have unusual scoring.
  You may get zero points for a question you don't answer, but *negative* points for an answer you get wrong. On these tests, it is better not to guess unless you can narrow down your choices.

If you can easily cross off two or more wrong answer choices, you can probably guess the correct answer. If you cannot narrow down the choices, skip the question.

Knowing the point value of a question helps you decide:

- which questions to answer first
- how to best use your time
- whether it's a good or bad idea to skip a question entirely

Think About It

With a big project, how do you decide what to do first, next, and last?

....

....

Budget Time

Just like budgeting money, you can budget time. For a test, start with the time you know you have to budget. This includes time to preview the question types and read directions. You also need time to figure out point values. Budget time, before the end of the test, to review and check your answers.

Lisa created this pie chart to visualize how to budget her time for the test. On a one-hour test, Lisa might spend six minutes previewing and six minutes reviewing. She would spend the remaining 48 minutes on taking the test.

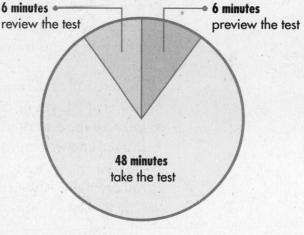

6 minutes review the test

6 minutes preview the test

48 minutes take the test

While Lisa didn't use the exact minutes for each part of the test, she knew about how much time to take. Budgeting time gives you a game plan. If something takes longer than budgeted, you have to decide what to do. Maybe you need to move on to the next section. Maybe you need to cut down review time. Even if you adjust it, just having a game plan will help you do better on a test.

Work with a Partner

Suppose you are taking a one-hour test. On this test there are:

- 10 true-false questions worth 1 point each
- 10 multiple-choice questions worth 3 points each
- 10 short-answer questions worth 6 points each

Fill in the pie chart below, marking how much time you will spend on each part of the test. Remember that you have 60 minutes in all to budget. Compare your pie chart to your partner's. How are they different? How are they the same? Discuss your reasons for dividing up the time the way you did.

preview = ... minutes

true-false = ... minutes

multiple-choice = ... minutes

short-answer = ... minutes

review = ... minutes

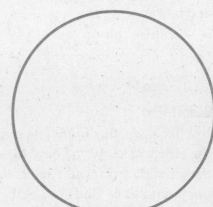

Review the Test

Budget a few minutes to review the test. As you check your answers, you can gain points by making sure you have:

- answered all of the questions
- answered everything completely
- followed the directions
- marked and written your answers clearly

If you cover all of these in a review, you have a good chance of doing well on the test.

Kelly wanted to be well prepared for an upcoming test. Before the test, she made her own checklist for reviewing it.

- ☻ Have I answered every question?
- ☻ Did I follow the directions?
- ☻ Do my math answers match my estimates?
- ☻ Did I spell words correctly?
- ☻ Is my grammar correct?
- ☻ Have I used punctuation marks correctly?
- ☻ Is my handwriting easy to read?
- ☻ Does my essay respond completely to the prompt?
- ☻ Are my answers clearly marked on the form?
- ☻ Have I erased any stray marks?
- ☻ Is there time to rework any difficult questions?

Try It Yourself

Create your own checklist to help you remember what to review.

....

....

....

....

Think About It

What kind of test questions take you the longest to answer?

....

....

TIP

Don't second-guess yourself as you review the test. Usually, your first answer will be the correct answer.

When You Take a Test

- Spend some time previewing question types and directions.
- Understand the point values of different questions.
- Manage your time during the test. Budget time for previewing and reviewing.

Journal

Write a paragraph about what you might do differently the next time you take a test. Try to be as specific as possible when you write.

Next, look at the goals you set on page 7. Note your progress for each of your goals. If you've achieved a goal, put a check next to it and congratulate yourself!

Topic 4: Review the Test

In this section, you will learn how to:
- *review your graded test*
- *revise your study plan*

Once the test is over, you'll probably feel a sense of relief. You did the best you could, and now it's out of your hands. But the test can still give you some valuable help. Once you get it back, you can use it to prepare for future tests.

Strategy 1: Review Your Graded Test

When you get the test back, go over it carefully. Check each section to see where you made mistakes. By looking at your errors, you can figure out how to do better on the next test.

People make mistakes. Some common reasons for errors on tests are

- reading the wrong material or not completing the reading
- reading the material but failing to understand it completely
- reading the test question but failing to understand it completely
- putting your answer in the wrong place or filling in the wrong oval on the answer form
- failing to remember facts and details; sometimes this is due to stress or exhaustion
- running out of time

An error chart, like the one below, can help you analyze the errors you made on a test. The first two columns show some common causes of errors and what they mean. Once you identify the errors, you can complete the last column by writing suggestions for the next time you take a test. This will help you avoid making the same mistakes again.

TIP
If your teacher's comments on the test are unclear, ask for an explanation.

Look at how Lisa completed the last column.

Cause of Error	What It Means	What I Can Do
lack of information	I never learned this information; I did not have it in my notes.	• Make sure I understand the main idea of each lecture or reading assignment. • Work with my instructor or other students to make sure I know what is most important.
loss of memory	I couldn't remember this information.	• Get enough sleep before a test! • Think about how I learn best. Make flash cards or tape record important information.
misunderstanding	I misunderstood this information when I read it or heard it.	• Ask questions in class. • Work with other students to check that we all understand things the same way.
reading problem	I misread the question or was unable to understand it.	• Take more time to preview questions and directions. • Think of ways to improve my reading skills.
vocabulary problem	I did not know the meaning of a key word in the question.	• Start keeping a journal of new vocabulary words. • Highlight or make a list of key terms as I read.
recording problem	I knew the answer but recorded it in the wrong place.	• Leave time to check answers against questions. • Don't get flustered!
time issue	I did not have time to answer the question fully; I did not have time to check my answers.	• Practice taking timed tests or writing against the clock. • Remember to budget time at the beginning of the test and stick to it.

Work with a Group

For each type of error on the chart, write in one or two things you could do to avoid such errors in the future. After everyone is done, compare notes in the group. What ideas from others can you use when taking a test?

Cause of Error	What I Can Do
lack of information	
loss of memory	
misunderstanding	
reading problem	
vocabulary problem	
recording problem	
time issue	

Think About It

Think about an area of your life where you have made mistakes. What have you learned from those past mistakes?

....

....

Strategy 2: Revise Your Study Plan

You've looked at your errors and decided how to fix them. Now it's time to revise and make a new study plan. These steps will help.

STEP 1   Think about what you did to study for this test. Think about what worked and what didn't work. You may need to change your study habits.

STEP 2   Review the ideas on how to choose a study plan. This was Strategy 2 of Topic 1 on pages 10–12. Figure out which ideas might work for you next time.

TIP

As you review your test, think about what did work as well as what did not. Keep what worked well for you.

STEP 3   Use the diagram below to decide what to do differently the
next time you study. By making a new study plan, you could
do better on your next test.

IF you worked alone before, ⟶ THEN should you find a
study group?

IF you misunderstood the material or studied the wrong things,
⟶ THEN should you ask more questions in class?

IF most of the tested material came from reading material rather
than lectures, ⟶ THEN should you take better notes on
the reading?

IF your notes were inadequate, ⟶ THEN should you try
using outlines?

Try It Yourself

Look back at your error chart from page 44. Think about what you
should change in your study plan. Write three things you could do
differently next time. How will these changes improve your test taking?

....

....

....

....

....

....

....

....

Think About It

Are there errors you commonly make on tests? What can you do to improve in the future?

....

....

....

When You Review a Test

- Look over your errors to see what you could do better.
- Revise your study plan based on what you learn.

Journal

Write a short paragraph describing three things you would look for when reviewing a test you took. Then write a short paragraph describing steps you could take to do better next time.

Next, look at the goals you set on page 7. Note your progress for each of your goals. If you've achieved a goal, put a check next to it and congratulate yourself!

What Works for You?

Are your test preparation habits changing? Review the test preparation habits you marked on page 5 and answer the questions.

How have my test preparation habits changed?

What test preparation habits do I want to work on?

Look at goals you set on page 7. Have you met your goals for test preparation? Answer the questions.

Which goals have I achieved so far?

Which goals do I want to work on?

Journal
Think about how you would help another person prepare for a test. Write a note to this friend in your journal. List some important ideas from this book that might help him or her.

Answers

Strategy 1: Answer Multiple-Choice Questions

Page 18: Work with a Partner

1. The movie *Titanic* is based on—
   - (A) an unsinkable ship—**wrong information**
   - (B) two people who are in love — **too narrow**
   - (C) a huge ship that sank with many lives lost—**correct**
   - (D) how weather affects sailing— **not relevant**
   - (E) a terrible tragedy in the 20th century—**too broad**

Page 20: Test Yourself

1. Ⓐ ⬤Ⓑ Ⓒ Ⓓ Ⓔ
2. ⬤Ⓐ Ⓑ Ⓒ Ⓓ Ⓔ
3. Ⓐ Ⓑ ⬤Ⓒ Ⓓ Ⓔ

Page 23: Try It Yourself

1. A is a correct answer, but so is B—so the answer is D.
2. Neither A, B, C, nor D is a possible answer—so the answer is E.
3. Only A is a correct answer.
4. Only A is a correct answer.

Strategy 2: Read Critically

Pages 26–27: Test Yourself

1. C (main idea)
2. B (vocabulary)
3. E (author's point of view)

Strategy 3: Respond to True-False Statements

Page 28: Test Yourself

1. T
2. F
3. T
4. T
5. T

Strategy 5: Answer Short-Answer Questions

Page 32: Try It Yourself

1. The Korean War took place *when*.
2. The first president of the United States was *who*.
3. The current president of the United States lives *where*.

Page 34: Test Yourself

1. Smokeless tobacco can damage teeth by exposing the roots of teeth and wearing down their surfaces.
2. Smokeless tobacco users often develop cancers on their lips, tongue, and gums.
3. Some baseball players have bulging cheeks because they hold wads of chewing tobacco between their teeth and gums.